1986

Wolfgang Amadeus Mozart

By
KARL BARTH

Foreword by
John Updike

Translated by
Clarence K. Pott

Grand Rapids, Michigan
William B. Eerdmans Publishing Company

Copyright © 1986 by Wm. B. Eerdmans Publishing Co.
255 Jefferson Ave. SE, Grand Rapids, Mich. 49503

Translated from *Wolfgang Amadeus Mozart, 1756/1956*
© 1956 by Theologischer Verlag Zürich

Library of Congress Cataloging in Publication Data

Barth, Karl, 1886-1968.
Wolfgang Amadeus Mozart.

English version of: Wolfgang Amadeus Mozart, 1756/1956.
1. Mozart, Wolfgang Amadeus, 1756-1791. 2. Composers
— Austria — Addresses, essays, lectures. I. Pott, C. K. II. Title.
ML410.M9B17913 1986   780'.92'4   85-29356

ISBN 0-8028-0007-6 (pbk.)

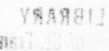

Contents

Foreword, John Updike   7

A Testimonial to Mozart   15

A Letter of Thanks to Mozart   19

Wolfgang Amadeus Mozart   25

Mozart's Freedom   43

5

Foreword

Karl Barth's insistence upon the otherness of God seemed to free him to be exceptionally (for a theologian) appreciative and indulgent of this world, the world at hand. His humor and love of combat, his capacity for friendship even with his ideological opponents, his fondness for his tobacco and other physical comforts, his tastes in art and entertainment were heartily worldly, worldly not in the fashion of those who accept this life as a way-station and testing-ground but of those who embrace it as a piece of Creation. The night of his death he was composing a lecture in which he wrote, in a tremulous but even hand, that "God is not a God of the dead but of the living"; not long before this Barth made notes foreseeing his death and the manifestation before "the judgment seat of Christ" of his "whole 'being,'" his being "with all the real good and the real evil that I have thought, said and done, with all the bitterness that I have suffered and all the beauty that I have enjoyed." Foremost for him in the ranks of beauty stood the music of Mozart, music which he placed, famously and almost notoriously, above the music of Bach and all others as a sounding-out of God's glory. He began each day with the playing of a Mozart record, partook of Mozart celebrations and festivals, and conscientiously served as a member of the Swiss Mozart Committee, which included the government minister Carl Burkhardt and the conductor Paul Sacher. "If I ever get to heaven," he said in the first tribute printed here, "I would first of all seek out Mozart."

It is good to have together, in this slim volume, Barth's formal pronouncements upon his — so to speak — idol, not only for the charm and ardor with which he addresses the subject but for what light his praise sheds upon that question which, despite all the voluminous Dogmatics and the superabundance of lectures, sermons, and incidental utterances that Barth's long and industrious life produced, remains a bit obscure in his version of Christianity: the question *What are we to do?* Granted that the situation of the world and of the individual life is as desperate as Barth paints it, and granted that the message of the Bible, and of the Pauline epistles in particular, is just as he explicates it, amid these radical truths how shall we conduct our daily and dim-sighted lives? Does not God's absolute otherness diminish to zero the significance of our petty activity and relative morality? Yet Mozart's activity, his *playing*, are regarded by Barth as exemplary, and the intensity and the *freedom* of Mozart's playing exonerate his narrowness, his ignorance of his era's science, politics, and philosophy, and the disastrous naïveté with which he conducted his practical affairs. Barth's attitude toward Mozart puts me in mind, incongruously, of Walt Whitman's praise, in "Song of Myself," of animals:

> They do not sweat and whine about their condition
> They do not lie awake in the dark and weep for their sins,
> They do not make me sick discussing their duty to God.

Like those beautiful and guiltless animals, Mozart's music says Yea; hearing it, Barth tells us, "one can live." By focusing so purely, so simply, upon the making of music, Mozart, like Whitman's panther who "walks to and fro on a limb overhead," gives us an example of tending to business, of channelling and reflecting, within the specialized talent, divine energy. Mozart, superb creature, "never knew doubt." His "ever-present lightness" exalts him above all other composers; Barth marvels at "how this man, while truly mastering his craft and always striving toward greater refinement, nevertheless manages never to *burden* his listeners — especially not with his creative labors!"

And yet a Yea, to have weight and significance for us, must contain and overpower a Nay, and so in Mozart's limpid outpouring Barth also hears "something very demanding, disturbing, almost provocative, even in the most radiant, most childlike, most joyful movements." "What he translated into music was real life in all its discord." His music reflects the conflicts and passions of his time as fully as the omnivorous mind of Goethe. A tireless absorber of the musical currents around him, Mozart "moved freely within the limits of the musical laws of his time, and then later ever more freely. But he did not revolt against these laws; he did not break them." It is in his consideration of Mozart's freedom that Barth becomes most theological, most instructive, and even most musicological: this ideal man, Mozart, carrying the full baggage of human woe and of temporal convention and restraint, possesses his freedom through a "triumphant turn" out of Nay into Yea. This turn is construed as more admirable than Goethe's sovereign humanism or Schleiermacher's location of a neutral center whereupon balance can be achieved: "What occurs in Mozart is rather a glorious upsetting of the balance, a turning in which the light rises and the shadows fall, though without disappearing, in which joy overtakes sorrow without extinguishing it, in which the Yea rings louder than the ever-present Nay."

"Though without disappearing" — thus the theologian acknowledges the inextinguishable problem of evil. He implies a cosmic paradigm in the way in which Mozart sweeps into his magnificent lightness everything problematical, painful, and dark. Mozart's music, for Barth, has the exact texture of God's world, of divine comedy. Hearing it, he is "transported to the threshold of a world which in sunlight and storm, by day and by night, is a good and ordered world." The order is, in Mozart, deeply assimilated and not a kind of exoskeleton, a message, as in Bach. Nor is Mozart engaged in personal confession, like Beethoven. Between the formal and the personal, he embodies the vital, the "living God" so recurrent in Barth's phraseology: Mozart's music, like the teeming drama of the Bible and like good crisis theology, gives us permission to live. "With an ear open to your musical dialectic, one can be young and become old, can work and rest, be content and sad: in short, one can live": thus Barth speaks directly to Mozart, in a tone of profound gratitude. Those who have not felt the difficulty of living have no need of Barthian theology; but then perhaps they also have no ear for music.

—JOHN UPDIKE

Wolfgang Amadeus Mozart

A Testimonial to Mozart

What sort of brief testimonial would I give to Mozart? A testimonial to a person and his work is a personal matter, and so I am glad to be able to speak personally. After all, I am not a musician or a musicologist. But I can — indeed I must — testify to my devotion to Mozart.

My very first hearing of great music — I must have been about five or six years old — was of Mozart. I can still recall: my father struck a few measures of *The Magic Flute* on the piano ("Tamino mine, oh what happiness"). They thrilled me through and through. Since then I have become older, and, finally, old. I have heard many more and very different things by Mozart, and he has become more and more of a constant in my life.

I have sometimes been asked whether, if I were to have proceeded on the basis of my theology, I should not have discovered quite different masters in music. I must insist (like those Indians from Orinoco whose first hearing of European music we have read about recently): no, it is Mozart and no one else. I confess that thanks to the invention of the phonograph, which can never be praised enough, I have for years and years begun each day with Mozart, and only then (aside from the daily newspaper) turned to my *Dogmatics*. I even have to confess that if I ever get to heaven, I would first of all seek out Mozart and only then inquire after Augustine, St. Thomas, Luther, Calvin, and Schleiermacher.

How am I to explain this? In a few words perhaps this way: our daily bread must also include playing. I hear Mozart — both younger and older — at play. But play is something so lofty and demanding that it requires mastery. And in Mozart I hear an art of playing as I hear it in no one else. Beautiful playing presupposes an intuitive, childlike awareness of the essence or center — as also the beginning and the end — of all things. It is from this center, from this beginning and end, that I hear Mozart create his music. I can hear those boundaries which he imposed upon himself because it was precisely this discipline that gave him joy. And when I hear him, it gladdens, encourages, and comforts me as well. Not that I want to utter even one critical word against anyone else. But in this sense I can offer my testimonial to Mozart alone.

From the Round Robin in the Neue Zürcher Zeitung, *Sunday, February 13, 1955*

A Letter of Thanks to Mozart

Basel, December 23, 1955

My dear Maestro and Court Composer:

Well now, someone hit upon the curious idea of inviting me and a few others to write for his newspaper a "Letter of Thanks to Mozart." At first I shook my head, my eye already on the waste basket. But since it is *you* who is to be the subject, I find it almost impossible to resist. For that matter, didn't you yourself write more than one rather odd letter during your lifetime? Well, then, why not me? To be sure, there where you are now — free of space and time — you [and your companions] know more about each other and also about us than is possible for us here. And so I don't doubt, really, that you have known for a long time how grateful I have been to you, grateful for as long as I can recall, and that this gratitude is constantly being renewed. But even so, why shouldn't you for once see this gratitude expressed in black and white?

But first, two preliminary matters. The first is that I am one of those Protestants of whom you are supposed to have once said that we probably could not properly understand the *Agnus Dei, qui tollis peccata mundi.* Pardon me — you probably know better now. Still, I don't want to trouble you with theology on this point. Imagine, rather, that I was dreaming about you last week, specifically that I was supposed to give you an examination (why is a mystery to me) and that to my question what "Dogmatics" and "Dogma" might mean, I received no answer at all — despite my most friendly prompting and my hints about your masses, which I especially like! This saddened me (because, after all, I knew that under no circumstances would you be allowed to fail). Shall we just let this matter rest?

There is another much more difficult problem. I have read that even when you were still a child, only the praise of experts could please you. As you know, there are on this earth not only musicians but also musicologists. You yourself were both; I am neither. I do not play an instrument, and I haven't the vaguest idea of the theory of harmony or of the mysteries of counterpoint. I am genuinely afraid, especially of those musicologists whose books about you I am trying to decipher, since I am composing a festival address for your birthday. Moreover, when I read the conclusions of these scholars, I fear that if I were young and could undertake this study, I should clash with several of your most important academic interpreters, just as I did with my theological mentors forty years ago. But be that as it may, how can I under these circumstances thank you as an expert and, as such, satisfy you?

Still, to my relief I have also read that you sometimes played hours on end for very simple people, merely because you sensed that they enjoyed listening to you. This is the way I have always heard you and still do, with constantly renewed enjoyment of ear and heart. I do this so naively that I cannot even be sure which of the thirty-four periods into which Wyzewa and St. Foix have divided your life and work appeals to me most. One thing is certain: that around 1785 you began to be truly great. But surely you won't be offended if I confess that it wasn't *Don Giovanni* and your later symphonies, not *The Magic Flute* and the *Requiem*, that first captivated me. I was deeply moved already by the "Haffner" Serenade and the Eleventh Divertimento, etc. — even by *Bastien and Bastienne.* Thus you became fascinating and dear to me even before you were hailed as the forerunner of Beethoven! What I thank you for is simply this: Whenever I listen to you, I am transported to the threshold of a world which in sunlight and storm, by day and by night, is a good and ordered world. Then, as a human being of the twentieth century, I always find myself blessed with courage (not arrogance), with tempo (not an exaggerated tempo), with purity (not a wearisome purity), with peace (not a slothful peace). With an ear open to your musical dialectic, one can be young and become old, can work and rest, be content and sad: in short, one can live.

Of course, you now know better than I that for *this* more than even the best music is needed. Still, there is music which as a supplement, and quite incidentally, helps us toward that life, and other music which helps us less. Your music helps. Because it is part of my life experience — in 1956 I shall be seventy, whereas you would now be walking among us as a 200-year-old patriarch! — and because I believe that in its growing darkness our age needs your help — for these reasons I am grateful that you walked among us, that in the few short decades of your life you wanted only to make pure music and that in your music you are still vitally with us. Please believe me: many many ears and hearts, both learned and as simple as mine, still love to listen to you again and again — and not only in your anniversary year!

What the state of music is where you are now I can only faintly surmise. Once upon a time I formulated my notion in this way: it may be that when the angels go about their task of praising God, they play only Bach. I am sure, however, that when they are together *en famille,* they play Mozart and that then too our dear Lord listens with special pleasure. Well, the contrast may be wrong, and of course you know more about this than I. I mention it only as a figure of speech to suggest what I mean.

And so, truly yours,

K. BARTH

From the Round Robin in the weekly supplement of the Luzerner Neuesten Nachrichten, *January 21, 1956*

Wolfgang Amadeus Mozart

The baptismal register of the cathedral church in Salzburg reports in 1756 "that Johannes Chrysostomus Wolfgang Theophilus, son of the Honorable Leopold Mozart, court musician, and Maria Anna Pertlin, his wife, was born at eight o'clock in the evening of January 27, 1756, and was baptized according to the Catholic sacrament at ten o'clock in the morning of January 28, 1756." Of the four stately names of this infant, the first together with the third might remind of another Johann Wolfgang, who was born seven years earlier in Frankfurt; the first plus the second recalls the church father Johannes, who, because of the loveliness of his teachings, received the name Chrysostomus (i.e., "Golden Mouth"). Only the last two names have become universally known and used, the fourth (Theophilus, or "Beloved of God") in the Latinized form Amadeus, usually changed by its bearer to "Amade."

Note first that the renowned man who is now to be commemorated in the Zwingli Almanac was born and baptized a Catholic and died a Catholic with last rites. That he became a Freemason in the last decade of his life certainly did not detract anything from whatever he thought he found in the Catholic worship and only in it (though without much churchly zeal). Given these facts, he could not really appreciate us Protestants because we had our religion ("whether there is any truth in that I wouldn't know") too much "in our head." Zwingli, taking into account the curious Christendom of Mozart's day, would probably have granted him a unique, direct access to God, which, to be sure, he granted even to all kinds of virtuous pagans. In the case of Mozart, we must certainly assume that the dear Lord had a special, direct contact with *him*. "He who has ears, let him hear!"

However, no one ought to suppose that it is easy to know with whom and what we are dealing here. Mozart's rich work, together with his brief, busy life, can never be satisfactorily accounted for; one could say it is a mystery. We must recognize this if we are to understand why his music (and in his music his person also) is to this day so moving.

Whoever has discovered Mozart even to a small degree and then tries to speak about him falls quickly into what seems rapturous stammering. This happened to Søren Kierkegaard, who threatened one time to "stir up the entire church from custodian to consistory" to get them to recognize that among all the great men, Mozart was the greatest. Failing that, he would "take his leave," sever relations with "their communion," and found a sect "which would not only exalt Mozart but honor *only* him." But, then, had not the reserved Goethe already characterized Mozart as a "miracle" unequalled in music? And did not countless other less famous people think the same thing, so that even in informed comparisons of Mozart with many earlier or later masters, words such as "unique," "incomparable," "perfect" crossed their minds and lips?

No doubt there is something in all this. If only one could say precisely what! Actually, it could be that in praising Mozart one really means Beethoven or Schubert, whose best work he anticipated in large measure in the music of his last days. Or in speaking of Mozart's work in the youthful and middle periods, one is really speaking of his appropriating one of the style forms of the eighteenth century, which was so unbelievably rich in musical invention. Just as happened in Old and New Testament scholarship, extensive efforts have been made of late to analyze Mozart's entire output from the perspective of the many impulses he received and assimilated in his earlier and later years: from the sons of Bach and, later, from Bach himself, from Handel and Gluck, from Joseph and Michael Haydn, but also from various German, Italian, and French composers now scarcely remembered. Was he perhaps unique in that he did not at all want to be an innovator, a revolutionary, or someone special? Is it possible that he could and wished to live and compose only out of the musical currents of his time and then, to be sure, in so doing translate his own unmistakable genius into music — that he could be, and wished to be, only a pupil, but as such "incomparable" and an absolute master? And the music of *his* time? Could it be that the characteristic basic "sound" of both the earlier and the later Mozart — not to be confused with the sound of any other — is in fact the primal sound of music absolutely? Could it be that he discovered and struck this "tone" in its timelessly valid form? And is that perhaps why it is so hard, even impossible, to define what is Mozartean —

no matter where you look and listen!? And is that why we have to resort to helpless superlatives when we try to explain this man to ourselves and to others?

It has been said that it is a child (a "divine" child to be sure), the "eternal youth," who speaks to us in his music. Perhaps it is the sad brevity of his earthly life that prompts this characterization—perhaps also the undeniable naiveté with which he conducted all practical affairs (according to his sharply critical sister, it became particularly evident on the occasion of his marriage and certainly in financial matters). Or is it perhaps because of the pranks and nonsense in which he indulged in his conversations and especially in his letters even during his final days? Yet, according to trustworthy accounts, these irrelevancies occurred most often precisely when he was hardest at work. No doubt we come nearer the truth (i.e., if we insist on regarding him as a "child"—Jacob Burckhardt one time protested strongly against doing so) when we consider how this man, while truly mastering his craft and always striving toward greater refinement, nevertheless manages never to *burden* his listeners—especially not with his creative labors! Rather, he always allows them to participate afresh in his free, let us now say "childlike," play. And we come nearer still when we reflect that, as someone else said of him, he is able "just as an innocent child to move us to smiles and tears at one and the same moment without our daring to ask him how and why."

And now consider that this same Mozart was never in fact allowed to be a child in the literal sense of the word: at age three he is already at the keyboard, at four he plays his little pieces flawlessly, at five he is composing. All this time his father is teaching him Latin, Italian, French, arithmetic, and always, always music theory. At six he goes on his first concert tour and at seven his second, this time for three and a half years — to Paris, London, Amsterdam, and on the way home to Geneva, Lausanne, Bern, Zurich, Winterthur, and Schaffhausen! Between the ages of fourteen and seventeen — already busy composing operas, masses, symphonies, quartets — he makes three tours to Italy. And so on and on! A child? No, a true *Wunderkind*, with hat and rapier (as Goethe saw him in Frankfurt in 1763), constantly performing and creating, adulated and decorated by the great Maria Theresa, by the kings of France and England (not to mention Madame de Pompadour), examined by musical experts, elevated by Pope Clement XIV to a "knighthood" and to a learned society in Bologna! All this under the management of his shrewd and zealous father (for him the lad came "second only to the dear Lord").

Father Leopold was convinced that developing this son's "talent" and spreading his fame was only proper and necessary — all to the honor of God (and, incidentally, with the complete assent and cooperation of the little man himself!). How appalling to Swiss ears: the benefits of school attendance were withheld from, or rather spared, little "Wolferl"! He had too many other things to do! It may be that the origins of the unknown illness from which he died before he was even thirty-six are to be sought in this unusual childhood. Also, it is a wonder that he did not develop into a vain little fop — again perhaps because he simply couldn't find the time for it. In any case, he never was a child in the ordinary sense. But, then, this was the price for being a "child" in that other, higher sense of the word. We must always keep this in mind lest we think and say something foolish.

There was a time when people were fond of characterizing Mozart's music as "charming" or "gay." He was the harbinger of an ever joyous rococo; he was even a kind of sun-god. Friedrich Theodor Fröhlich (1803 – 1836), the Swiss director of music at Aarau, who likewise died young, has celebrated him as a "child of May" — "a blissful smile on his lips," strolling under "an eternally blue sky." That was not and is not Mozart — not his life and certainly not his music. To the question whether Mozart had been "happy," an English contemporary who had known him personally, answered flatly, "Never." One ought to reflect on that when one speaks of the "joy conferred by his music"! And also when one ponders the conjecture (actually more than a conjecture) that he was indeed in love often enough but never really loved any woman except Frau Musica. Then there were the sorrows occasioned by his later estrangement from his father, by his depressing circumstances in the service of the Archbishop Colloredo of Salzburg, by the recurring professional disappointments in Vienna, by his chronic financial troubles, and finally by his illness. Mozart laughed often, but surely not because he had much to laugh about. Rather — and this is something quite different — because he could and did laugh *despite* all these things.

It is also true — and this may be the real

truth to the legend of Mozart as the "child of May" — that, as a perceptive Frenchman of our century has expressed it, he never knew doubt. Herein is the strangely exciting but at the same time calming quality of his music: it evidently comes from on high, where (since everything is known there) the right and the left of existence and therefore its joy and sorrow, good and evil, life and death, are experienced in their reality but also in their limitation. Poor Hans Georg Nägeli (composer of *The Holiest of Nights!*), who attacked Mozart precisely for those contrasts which are so characteristic of his music! How could one so misunderstand him just in this respect? No, Mozart was not of sanguine temperament, not an optimist (not even in his most radiant major-key movements, not in his serenades and divertimenti, nor in *Figaro,* nor in *Cosi fan tutte!*). But no, neither was he a melancholic or a pessimist (not in the small or in the great G-Minor Symphonies, not in the D-Minor Piano Concerto, nor in the "Dissonance" Quartet, nor in the Overture to and the Finale of *Don Giovanni!*).

What he translated into music was real life in all its discord. But in defiance of that, and on the sure foundation of God's good creation, and because of that, he moves always from left to right, never the reverse. This, no doubt, is what is meant by his triumphant "charm." In Mozart there are no flat plains but no abysses either. He does not make things easy for himself. But neither does he let himself go; he is never guilty of excess. Imposing limits, he tells us how everything is. Therein lies the beauty of his beneficent and moving music. I know of no other about whom one can say quite the same thing.

Mozart is universal. One marvels again and again how everything comes to expression in him: heaven and earth, nature and man, comedy and tragedy, passion in all its forms and the most profound inner peace, the Virgin Mary and the demons, the church mass, the curious solemnity of the Freemasons and the dance hall, ignorant and sophisticated people, cowards and heroes (genuine or bogus), the faithful and the faithless, aristocrats and peasants, Papageno and Sarastro. And he seems to concern himself with each of these in turn not only partially but fully; rain and sunshine fall on all. This is reflected, I think, in the utterly lovely but always, it seems, effortless and inevitable way in which he shapes and arranges the relationship among human voices, or in the concertos between the reigning solo instrument and the accompanying strings and wind instruments — which never merely accompany. Can one ever listen enough to what happens in a Mozart orchestra, how the components are introduced, unexpected but always with perfect timing, in their own height or depth and tone color? It is as though in a small segment the whole universe bursts into song because evidently the man Mozart has apprehended the cosmos and now, functioning only as a medium, brings it into song! Truly, we can call this "incomparable."

But now we must note another riddle. According to everything we know of Mozart, he took no interest whatsoever in the flourishing natural science and historical study of his time, nor, aside from music, in its art or in classical literature. He possessed Goethe's poems, but his relationship to Goethe is reflected only in the "Song of the Violet" [*Das Veilchen*]. A reference to the death of Christian F. Gellert (he spells it "Gelehrt" in one of his youthful letters) and a humorous description of the poet Wieland, whom he happened to meet in Mannheim in 1777, are to my knowledge the only things he wrote about the literature of his day. And not even a trace of another contemporary by the name of Immanuel Kant! I do not know either of any passage in his letters which offers more than a passing impression of the landscape and architecture of his homeland and of those countries he traveled through. The charming picture of him which Mörike presents in the well-known novelle *Mozart auf der Reise nach Prag* [*Mozart's Journey to Prague*] may well be fiction rather than fact. And so it is probably love's labor lost to try to understand him from the background of old Salzburg and environs. The political events of his day, including the outbreak of the French Revolution, did not noticeably touch him. (Or should one at this point mention the anecdote of the six-year-old Mozart's meeting with the little archduchess Marie Antoinette, later the unhappy queen of France? She caught him as he slipped on the smooth parqueted floor of the Vienna court, whereupon the little Mozart promptly proposed marriage.) Aside from his changing human and professional concerns, he seems all his life, in fact, to have been attentive only to those matters connected with music. Question: How then did he know all things so clearly, as his music reveals? He knew them at least as vividly as Goethe, whose eye for nature, history, and art Mozart seemed not at all to possess — and unquestionably more clearly than hundreds of thousands of better read, better "educated," more interested connoisseurs of the world and of man in all ages. I do not know the answer. He must have had organs which, as if to belie that extraordinary seclusion from the external world, made it in fact possible for him to apprehend universally what he was able to state universally.

Mozart's music is not, in contrast to that of Bach, a message, and not, in contrast to that of Beethoven, a personal confession. He does not reveal in his music any doctrine and certainly not himself. The discoveries ostensibly made in both these directions, especially in his later works, seem to me artificial and not very illuminating. Mozart does not wish to *say* anything: he just sings and sounds. Thus he does not force anything on the listener, does not demand that he make any decisions or take any positions; he simply leaves him free. Doubtless the enjoyment he gives begins with our accepting that. On one occasion he called death man's true best friend, and he thought daily of death, as his works plainly reveal. But he does not dwell on it unduly; he merely lets us discover it. Nor does he *will* to proclaim the praise of God. He just does it — precisely in that humility in which he himself is, so to speak, only the instrument with which he allows us to hear what he hears: what surges at him from God's creation, what rises in him, and must proceed from him.

A word about his church music, often criticized by serious scholars. Too worldly, indeed operatic, it is repeatedly called — with the rather feeble explanation that here Mozart follows the general mode of his time. This much is true: in the music he contributed to this area, he did not really observe the well-established norm that the music should only serve the Word and explain it. But is that the only possible principle for church music? After all, Mozart did not adhere to such rules in his operas either. If I hear him rightly, in his church music as in all his other creations, the music is a free counterpart to that word given him. This is what inspires him, this is what he accompanies and plays about. The sound corresponds to it — and, yes, this does mean that in relation to the word, his music takes on a life of its own. But in each case it is always *this* music which corresponds to *this* word, always *this* composition to *this* text and no other. His music for Freemasons could not be that of his *Requiem*. Conversely, he could not possibly allow the soprano in the C-Minor Mass to sing the same music for the *Laudamus te* or the *Et incarnatus est* as, for example, the page in *Figaro* where Figaro sings, "You who know the impulses of the heart," and the like. This is so even though he unmistakably gives the same color to both. In both he hears and respects the word in its distinctive form and character, but then to both he sets his own music — a music bound by the word but in this "binding" still a sovereign shape with its own nature. We ought to ask whether this music in this relationship is in each case appropriate to the word, also when it is a question of sacred texts (and not prejudiced by a general distinction between sacred and secular music). Then we shall surely discover more and more that the music in this relationship is most appropriate to the objective statements of the sacred texts — to be sure, often in a very surprising way. This is perhaps because Mozart's sacred music, too, is heard to originate in a region from which vantage point God and the world are certainly not to be judged identical but which does allow church and world (these also not to be interchanged) to be recognizable

and recognized in their merely relative differ-
ence, in their ultimate togetherness: both ema-
nating from God, both going back to God.

A final sad thought. Considering how brief his
life was, the number of Mozart's preserved works
is enormous. But probably even greater is the
number of all those works of which we are de-
prived and destined to remain so. We know that
at all periods of his life he loved to improvise,
i.e., to freely create and play for himself either
in public concerts or hours on end to only a
small audience. What he did in this way was not
written down—a whole Mozartean world that
sounded once and then faded away forever!

What did he look like? Certainly not as de-
picted on most of the preserved portraits; they
all seem to suggest the sun-god. On internal and
external grounds, the unfinished oil portrait of
1782 by Mozart's brother-in-law Joseph Lange
may come closest to the truth. He had blue eyes,
a pointed and rather longish nose. According to
the description of still another Englishman, he
was "an extraordinarily small man, very thin and
pale, with a mass of beautiful blond hair of which
he seemed proud." For the rest, he was fond of
billiards, dancing, and—punch: "I saw him con-

sume large quantities of this drink." Not an immediately impressive character! Who and what he was must ordinarily have been quite invisible — to become visible for the first time (and then, perhaps, only *audible*) when he sat down at the keyboard. And then he became the consummately great Wolfgang Amadeus Mozart. Let us be grateful that he is available to us at least as a mighty echo of what once was.

From the Zwingli-Kalender *(Basel: Friedrich Reinhardt, 1956)*

41

Mozart's Freedom

Address delivered on the occasion of the Commemorative Celebration in the Music Hall in Basel on January 29, 1956.

Esteemed Ladies and Gentlemen!

Let me begin with a few words uttered in 1768 by the musical director of the Archbishopric of Salzburg, Leopold Mozart, the father. He had conducted his children, twelve-year-old "Nannerl" and seven-year-old "Wolferl," on a three-and-a-half-year concert tour through all of western Europe. And now the brilliance of the boy's art and technique in performance and composition was to be displayed in the imperial city of Vienna. There were difficulties. Referring to them, the father writes that he was anxious "to announce to the world *a miracle which God had been pleased to perform in Salzburg. I owe this to Almighty God; otherwise I should be the most* ungrateful creature.... Was it not a great joy and triumph for me when I heard a Voltairean tell me in astonishment, I have now for the first time in my life seen a miracle." The Voltairean was the Encyclopedist Friedrich Melchior Grimm, who had heard "Wolferl" in Paris in 1763 and who actually did say at the time: "I truly fear that this child will turn my head if I hear him again; he has shown me how difficult it is to preserve one's sanity in the face of a miracle." And later, did not the aged Goethe also characterize the phenomenon of Mozart as a "miracle," with nothing more to be said? One might have thought that whether by a Christian believer like father Mozart or by an unbeliever like Baron Grimm or even by a Goethe the term "miracle" could have been used a bit more sparingly. Still, how many others have uttered similar things in other words about Wolfgang Amadeus Mozart! I find it striking how often especially other musicians of note — during Mozart's lifetime Joseph Haydn, later Rossini, Gounod, Busoni, and in our own lifetime Arthur Honegger and Ernest Ansermet (all deserving our profound respect) — can manage only a kind of ecstatic stammer when it comes to speaking of this fellow artist. I don't wish to follow their example here. Likewise, I leave open the question, quietly suggested to me not long ago by a well-known contemporary, whether Mozart could possibly have been an angel. No, I mention all this only to remind ourselves that when we are dealing with the life and work of the man we are commemorating today, we are dealing with something exceedingly special. What was, and is, this particular marvel?

Two riddles in the phenomenon that is Mozart may point the way to an answer.

The first is this: When we listen to Mozart we are introduced to all of eighteenth-century music. Was there ever a musician who at all stages of his career was so receptive to the attempts and achievements of predecessors and contemporaries, major and minor? Receptive also to the entire world of melody in his surroundings, from the sacred chorale down to the Vienna street song? We know that while composing he was not at all disturbed — rather it spurred him on — if there was singing in the room next door, piano playing below, clarinet playing above, and maybe even bowling in the street outside. And even in his last years, he studied Bach and Handel with the earnestness of a beginner. In the most diverse places in his works one must be prepared for reminiscences and quotations. To this day, not only minor but also highly respected Mozart scholars are quite capable of confusing his work with that of others. And in certain works, rightly or wrongly attributed to him, there is always the doubt: Are they really his? But then the eighteenth century is not just Mozart and Mozart is not just the eighteenth century. For amidst all the styles, manners, and motifs which he took over, there is already in the keyboard pieces of the child — if only we could define it precisely! — a certain preeminent Mozartean sound. What was originally foreign to him, until he made it his own, became in his ears, in his head and spirit, and under his hands something which it had not been before: it became — Mozart. Even while he adapted, and precisely then, the man was creative. He certainly never merely imitated. From the beginning, he moved freely within the limits of the musical laws of his time, and then later ever more freely. But he did not revolt against these laws; he did not break them. He sought to be himself and yet achieved his greatness precisely in being himself while observing the conventions which he imposed upon himself. We must be aware of both these elements together. This is the mystery behind which we must seek his special genius if we are to appreciate the superiority with which he moved within his artistic and human surroundings. To this day he seems to us an eagle soaring above the concert hall.

The other riddle lies deeper. Mozart's music always sounds unburdened, effortless, and light. This is why it unburdens, releases, and liberates us. This is so in his famous minor-key compositions; this is so when he composes *opera seria* — even in the sacred works culminating in the *Requiem,* even in the Freemason melodies, even when he becomes solemn, melancholy, and tragic. But he never becomes truly tragic. He plays and never stops playing, and the listener who does not himself sway and soar, who does not play along with him, is not truly hearing him. But neither is one truly hearing him if, as happened in the nineteenth century, he is heard as a musician of mere facile gaiety. Behind his play there is an iron zeal. How the man worked during his short lifetime: during his journeys or in the company of others or simply playing billiards, with melodies singing in his head, shaping, unfolding, and integrating and bringing them out complete in an unceasing flood, as though he were simply writing letters — that was his prodigious achievement! And all this no matter whether he was improvising on the keyboard for many listeners or few, or alone in the solitude of the night. Surely this explains also why his music — how foolish to speak of ease here — is not effortlessly accessible, why this ever-present lightness possesses something very demanding, disturbing, almost provocative, even in the most radiant, most childlike, most joyful movements. If one cannot sense this, then indeed one cannot experience release from listening to Mozart. No doubt this is also why, in singing, playing, and directing Mozart properly, the performing artist, as has been attested, faces a beautiful task but also one of the most demanding. It is indeed true, as I found it happily expressed recently, "His gravity soars and his lightness is infinitely grave." I wonder whether one could say quite the same thing of any other musician — indeed, everything considered, *must* say this? In any case, Mozart's specific genius might be associated also with this paradox — except that in him it is not a paradox.

Let me now say something about what I should like to call the great, free "objectivity" with which Mozart went through life. His significant experiences as a *man*, at least from the time he was twenty, were almost all dark and painful, albeit continually interspersed with and surrounded by small moments of brightness, joy, and even gaiety. Why, even through the fevers of the night he died (December 4 – 5, 1791), wasn't he still busy with his *Requiem* and wasn't his mind also on his *Magic Flute*, being performed elsewhere during those very hours? But the *Requiem* is not his personal confession and neither is *The Magic Flute*. The subjective is never his theme. He never used music to express himself, his situation, his moods. I do not know of a single instance where one can with any certainty explain the character of a work from a corresponding episode in his life, so that from the succession of his works one might trace something like a biographical line. Mozart's life served his art, not the other way around, except in the prosaic sense that he had to support Frau Constanze and their children — money, alas, so quickly spent. When he set himself to executing those ever-welcome commissions, he himself, with wife and children (or in the past his sick mother, the faithless Aloysia Weber, his angry father, not to mention the wretched Archbishop Colloredo and Count Arco) — all were forgotten, consigned to a distant background, in favor of the task once again to give voice, quite oblivious to the important and the trivial experiences of his life, to that small part of the universe of sound in which he dwelt. What then came forth was always, and still is, an invitation to the listener to venture just a little out of the snail's shell of his own subjectivity.

Mozart the *artist* came a long way too, as one can learn from the most significant recent analysis of his work. He touched upon and used so many models throughout the thirty-four periods of his life as a composer. Following this journey must be an extraordinarily fascinating study for those who are knowledgeable about such matters. But we must not be captivated even by such excellent studies. For example, we should not be persuaded to listen seriously only to those works in which Mozart seems to approach Beethoven, as though Beethoven were the measure of all things. On his artistic journey, Mozart displays so many exceptions to the rule, he anticipates so much of later stages and revives so much of earlier ones, that we are wise to remain as open to the middle and early Mozart as we are to the later, who is so often praised as "classical." Consider, for example, what was possible for Mozart already in *Idomeneo* — and is still possible in *The Magic Flute*! In this regard, too, we discern a free Mozartean "objectivity." Whether in *this* earlier or *that* later stage, he heard the same sounding cosmos with the same ears. And in every instance, he never wished merely to display his technical prowess, but only to place himself at the service of Frau Musica, to whom he had dedicated himself from childhood. It is this *sovereign submission* at all stages of his artistic career which may be taken as a distinct feature of what was unique and special in the man.

And now, in our attempt to define this special quality, it may be appropriate to focus on the concept of *freedom* from still another direction. As performer and composer, Mozart always had something to say, and he said it. But we should not complicate and spoil the impact of his works by burdening them with those doctrines and ideologies which critics think they have discovered in them but which are in fact an imposition. There is in Mozart no "moral to the story," either mundane or sublime. He certainly consulted closely with the librettists for his operas, but not at all to arrive at some agreed-upon profound meaning! We must take to heart what he wrote to his father in 1781: "In an opera the poetry must absolutely be the obedient daughter of the music!" What this means is that neither Lorenzo da Ponte nor Emanuel Schikaneder gave him or collaborated with him on this or that earth-shaking theme — this to be set to music by him. What he wanted from them and discussed with them was the most fitting libretto to serve as impetus for the statement and development of his own decisively musical themes, motifs, dramas, and figurations. These were then developed into pure counterparts to the mediocre creations of these third- or fifth-rate authors. Thus, Mozart's *Figaro* has nothing to do with the ideas of the French Revolution, nor *Don Giovanni* with the myth of the Eternal Rake (Kierkegaard notwithstanding!). Nor is there a Mozartean "philosophy of *Cosi fan tutte*"; and we should not claim to hear much of a religious humanism or of other political mysteries when we listen to *The Magic Flute*. If we judge from his letters, the fact is simply — whether we like it or not — that he was never directly or specifically affected by nature around him or by the history, literature, philosophy, and politics of his time. With regard to these he had no special conclusions and theories to present and proclaim. I fear he did not read very much; he certainly never speculated or lectured. There is no Mozartean metaphysics. In the realms of nature and spirit, he sought for and found only the opportunities, materials, and tasks for his music. With God, the world, himself, heaven and earth, life — and, above all, death — ever present before his eyes, in his hearing, and in his heart, he was a profoundly unproblematical and thus a free man: a freedom, so it seems, *given* to him — indeed *commanded* and therefore exemplary for him.

This implies that to an extraordinary degree his music is free of all exaggeration, of all sharp breaks and contradictions. The sun shines but does not blind, does not burn or consume. Heaven arches over the earth, but it does not weigh it down, it does not crush or devour it. Hence earth remains earth, with no need to maintain itself in a titanic revolt against heaven. Granted, darkness, chaos, death, and hell do appear, but not for a moment are they allowed to prevail. Knowing all, Mozart creates music from a mysterious center, and so knows and observes limits to the right and the left, above and below. He maintains moderation. Again in 1781, he wrote that "passions, violent or not, may never be expressed to the point of revulsion, that even in the most frightening situation music must never offend the ear but must even then offer enjoyment, i.e., music must always remain music." As Grillparzer has said so beautifully, he was the musician "who never did too little and never too much, who always attains but never exceeds his goal." There is no light which does not also know dark, no joy which does not also have within it sorrow; but the converse is also true: no fear, no rage, no plaint which does not have, far or near, peace at its side. No laughter without tears, no weeping without laughter! There is no substance to the legend of a Mozart of pure grace, a legend so ardently proclaimed by the nineteenth century, which then, not unexpectedly, turned its back on him. But neither is there any substance to the "demonic Mozart" which our century wishes to substitute. It is precisely the absence of all demons, just this stopping short of extremes, just this wise confrontation and mixture of the elements which — once again — are the constituents of that freedom with which Mozart's music renders the true *vox humana* through the whole scale of its possibilities — unsubdued, but also undistorted and without convulsions. The true listener may regard himself as also called to this freedom — to see himself as the person he really is: as the cunning Basilio and the gentle Cherubino, as the hero Don Giovanni and the coward Leporello, as the tender Pamina and the raging Queen of the Night, as the all-forgiving countess and the terrifying, jealous Electra, as the wise Sarastro and the foolish Papageno. They lie hidden in all of us. He may see himself as still living but destined for the grave — as we all are.

One more thing must be noted and said. The Mozartean "center" is not like that of the great theologian Schleiermacher — a matter of balance, neutrality, and, finally, indifference. What occurs in Mozart is rather a glorious upsetting of the balance, a *turning* in which the light rises and the shadows fall, though without disappearing, in which joy overtakes sorrow without extinguishing it, in which the Yea rings louder than the ever-present Nay. Note the *reversal* of the great dark and the small light episodes in Mozart's life! At the conclusion of *The Magic Flute* we hear, "The rays of the sun *drive out* the night." The play can and must go on, or begin all over again. At some level, high or low, it is a contest to be won; actually it is already won. This fact gives it its direction and character. We will never hear in Mozart an equilibrium of forces and a consequent uncertainty and doubt. This is as true of his operas as of his instrumental music and especially so of his sacred works. In the latter, does not every *Kyrie*, every *Miserere*, no matter how darkly foreboding its beginning, sound as if borne upward by the trust that the plea for mercy was granted long ago? *Benedictus qui venit in nomine Domine*! In Mozart's version he evidently has already come. *Dona nobis pacem*! — a prayer, but a prayer already answered. This feature is enough to mark Mozart's church music as truly sacred, all objections notwithstanding. Mozart never lamented, never quarreled, though he certainly was entitled to. Instead, he always achieved this consoling turn, which for everyone who hears it is priceless. And that seems to me, insofar as one can say it at all, to be the secret of his *freedom* and with it the essence of Mozart's *special quality* which engaged our attention at the beginning.

In conclusion, a few loosely connected observations: There is a question which I shall leave unanswered, but which surely has not escaped you. How can I as an evangelical Christian and theologian proclaim Mozart? After all he was so Catholic, even a Freemason, and for the rest no more than a musician, albeit a complete one. He who has ears has certainly heard. May I ask all those others who may be shaking their heads in astonishment and anxiety to be content for the moment with the general reminder that the New Testament speaks not only of the kingdom of heaven but also of *parables* of the kingdom of heaven?

A few other points on which I shall comment briefly.

Mozart and other great musicians. Don't be afraid that I'll say something fanatical — that would be altogether un-Mozartean! It was Karl Friedrich Zelter, Goethe's consultant in music, who one day muttered testily to his great friend, "as though after Mozart no one ought to be allowed to compose, to die, or to find peace!" Certainly no one could or should be denied these. Yet, we might mention how one of Mozart's first biographers, Professor Franz Niemetschek, from Prague, formulated the matter, however hesitantly, seven years after Mozart's death: "Whoever has learned to love Mozart will find it hard to be really satisfied with other music."

Mozart and Goethe. It is more than probable that Mozart had not read him. He composed the "Song of the Violet" [*Das Veilchen*] without knowing that it was Goethe's. And Goethe, quite content with the efforts of his Zelter, seems not to have taken notice of Mozart's musical setting of his poem. For the rest, Goethe referred to the "incomparable genuis" of Mozart (unfortunately, we do not know in what sense), he mentioned him in the same breath with Raphael and Shakespeare, and he deemed only Mozart capable of setting his *Faust* to music. What experiences these two might have had if they had met! I find it hard to compare them, because the Mozartean *center* is not ultimately the same as the Goethean *sovereignty* and because that imbalance between the two opposing aspects of life which is so decidedly characteristic of Mozart — that triumphant turn, i.e., Mozart's *freedom* — does not, if I am correct, have any counterpart in Goethe.

Mozart and Basel. Basel is not a "Mozart-city" — so said a local newspaper this winter. Well yes, Basel is not Salzburg, not Prague, not Vienna; Basel is Basel. It may be true that Bach and Beethoven are more acclaimed here than is

Mozart. And I can not repress a terrible rec-
ollection: when the Mozart family, returning from
the great concert tour in the fall of 1766, jour-
neyed through Switzerland, the father preferred,
incomprehensibly, to travel to Salzburg not by
way of Basel but through Zurich, so that he
could present his prodigies in concert there rather
than in our city. Fortunately, that is a long time
ago. But if today a few hundred good souls in
Basel continue to cultivate an attentive ear for
Mozart's freedom, that might be enough to quietly make of Basel a "Mozart-city" after all.

Finally: *Mozart and the great painters*. Following
Goethe's example, others have also compared
Mozart's music with the paintings of Raphael. If
a comparison is to be made, I should venture
that it might be even more pertinent to contem-
plate the marvelously clear line, the unmistakable relationships and limits, especially the
unfathomable Knowing, Questioning, and An-
swering to be found in the human faces of the
paintings of Sandro Botticelli. As these eyes seem
to *see,* so Wolfgang Amadeus Mozart, in his
great freedom, may have *heard,* and then in this
same great freedom, have played as it was given
to him to play.

But now it is high time that as a conclusion to this festival we hear again from Mozart himself.

[The festival opened and concluded with the Serenade in C Minor (K. 388), performed by the Wind Chamber Ensemble of the Basel Orchestral Society, under the direction of Joseph Bopp. Barth's address was also given in Thun on January 27.]